THE WINTER OLYMPICS

A TRUE BOOK

by

Larry Dane Brimner

Children's Press®
A Division of Grolier Publishing

New York London Hong Kong Sydney
Danbury, Connecticut

Reading Consultant
Linda Cornwell
Learning Resource Consultant
Indiana Department
of Education

For Susie Ward,
librarian extraordinaire

Olympic flags fly during
the 1988 Winter Olympics
in Calgary, Canada.

Library of Congress Cataloging-in-Publication Data

Brimner, Larry Dane
    The Winter Olympics / by Larry Dane Brimner.
       p.   cm. — (A true book)
    Includes index.
    Summary: Briefly discusses the international competition in winter
sports, beginning with the Nordic Games in 1908, and describes some of
the sports involved, including skiing, ice hockey, skating, and bobsledding.
    ISBN 0-516-20456-4   (lib. bdg.)   0-516-26207-6 (pbk.)
    1. Winter Olympics—Juvenile literature. [1. Winter Olympics.] I. Title.
II. Series.
GV841.B75 1997
796.98—dc21   97-2272
                                              CIP
                                             AC

Contents

The opening ceremonies (top) welcome the athletes of the 1988 Winter Olympics at Calgary, Canada. Oksana Baiul (right) wears an Olympic athlete's highest award: a gold medal.

What Are the Olympic Winter Games?

Every four years, an amazing thing happens. Some of the world's best athletes gather in a place where the air is crisp and snow covers the ground. They are the athletes of winter—skiers, skaters, and sledders. They will compete at the Olympic Winter Games to set new records, win medals, and gain fame.

Athletes have been competing at the Olympic Winter Games since 1924. Before then, many of winter's athletes competed in the Nordic Games. The Nordic Games began in 1901 and were held every four years in Sweden.

In the 1908 Summer Olympics in London, England, figure skating was added to

The popularity of figure skating increased demand for a separate Olympics in the winter.

the schedule. The spectators loved it! Again, in 1920, figure skating returned to the Olympic schedule in Antwerp, Belgium, along with ice hockey. These events proved so popular that the International Olympic Committee (IOC) decided to stage a separate festival of winter sports. It would be called "International Sports Week 1924."

Who were the big winners of International Sports Week 1924? Athletes from Sweden and its Scandinavian neighbors took home most of the medals.

The IOC decided to make the winter festival a permanent event like the Summer Olympics. Because the 1924 winter festival marked the first

Winter Olympics, the IOC changed the festival's name. International Sports Week 1924 became known officially as the "First Olympic Winter Games." Since then, the Olympic Winter Games have been held every four years, except during World War II

Canada and the United States battle for the puck during the 1924 Winter Olympics.

(1939–45), when the Games were canceled. The only other exception has been the two-year gap between the 1992 and 1994 Winter Games. This was done so that future Winter Games would not be held in the same year as the Summer Olympics.

Can you name the winter sports?

The athletes of the XVIII (Eighteenth) Olympic Winter Games in Nagano, Japan, will compete in seven

For these Italian lugers and all Olympic athletes, making it to the Winter Olympics is a great victory.

different sports. They are skiing, skating, ice hockey, the biathlon, bobsledding, lugeing (or tobogganing), and curling. Playing for an Olympic team is very difficult. The athletes of the Winter Olympics represent the very best a country can offer.

Olympic Goals and Symbols

Both the Summer and Winter Olympics are about more than sports. They have a loftier goal. Pierre de Coubertin was the founder of the modern Olympics. He was inspired by the ancient Olympic Games of Greece. In ancient Greece, warring nations would lay down

The founder of the modern Olympics, Pierre de Coubertin (left). In ancient Greece, an athlete is crowned winner (right).

their weapons so that athletes could compete in peace. Pierre de Coubertin hoped that a modern Olympic Games would inspire peace among the nations of the world. He also felt that sports could encourage fair play, understanding, and friendship.

These have become the goals that govern the Olympics. They are captured in the Latin motto of the Olympics: Citius, Altius, Fortius. It means, "Faster, Higher, Braver."

You have probably seen the Olympic emblem—five connected rings in blue, yellow, black, green, and red. At least one of the colors is found on the flag of every country participating in the Olympics. The five rings represent the five parts of the world that united for the early Olympic

games. (The five parts were Europe, Asia, Africa, Oceania, and the Americas.) The linked rings also represent the Olympic spirit of togetherness and friendship.

The Olympic flame is another widely known symbol of the Olympics. During the ancient Olympic Games in Greece, a flame was kept burning on the

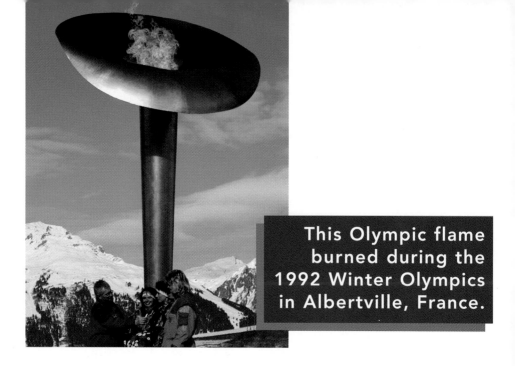

This Olympic flame burned during the 1992 Winter Olympics in Albertville, France.

altar of the goddess Hera. At the modern Games, a torch carried from Olympia, Greece, is used to ignite the Olympic flame during the opening cere-monies. The Olympic flame remains burning throughout the Games. It symbolizes the link between the past and present.

The Olympic Torch Relay

The Olympic torch relay is a tradition that began at the 1936 Berlin Games. The torch was lit at Olympia, Greece. From there, it was carried by three thousand runners. They crossed seven countries before arriving at the stadium and lighting the Olympic Flame in Berlin (above). Lighting of the Olympic Flame is filled with ceremony and spectacle. It is always a breathtaking event. At the XVII Olympic Winter Games in Lillehammer, Norway, Stein Gruben awed the crowd when he ski-jumped into the arena with the torch flaming (left).

Skiing and Biathlon

Skiing events consist of both Alpine and Nordic styles. What makes the two styles different? Alpine skiers ski downhill, while Nordic skiers ski jump or ski cross-country.

Alpine skiing is a race against other skiers and the clock. Alpine skiers zip down-

In Alpine or downhill
skiing, the fastest skier
to the bottom wins.

hill at speeds that sometimes reach 70 miles per hour (112.6 kilometers per hour) and greater. There are several different Alpine events. In the downhill event, the skier races down a mountain's slope. The skier with the fastest time wins the event. In the slalom, giant slalom, and the super giant slalom, racers speed downhill while making several turns at flags, or gates. The super giant slalom,

In slalom, the racer must ski between gates.

or super-G, is the longest, while the slalom is the shortest. The Alpine combined event does just what its name suggests. It combines a downhill race with two slalom runs.

Cross-country skiers travel over different kinds of terrain.

Nordic skiers, or cross-country racers, are like long-distance runners. Their races stretch out through valleys and meadows, and up and down hills. One event is 40 kilometers (24.8 miles) long, and another is staged over two days.

The biathlon began as a military exercise in 1767. It combines Nordic skiing and rifle shooting. Both skills were, and still are, important to soldiers patrolling snow-covered

During a biathlon, a skier carefully prepares to shoot at targets.

lands. It became part of the Olympics in 1960. The event requires each skier to follow a set course. Along the way, he or she must stop to shoot at targets—sometimes from a standing position and sometimes while lying down.

Ski jumping is another Nordic event. It started as a contest in 1862 in Norway, and it is one of the most spectacular events to watch. Skiers fly down a snow-

A ski jumper flies high above the crowd.

covered ramp (the "in-run") and launch into the air. They are judged on the jump's distance and style.

Hoping for a medal, this freestyle mogul skier (left) performs a stunt. Twists and flips make up aerial freestyle skiing (right).

Freestyle skiing was first seen in the Olympics as a demonstration event. Until the 1994 Games, it was customary to perform unusual sports as "demonstrations." This means that they were not eligible for Olympic medals. (Demonstration events are no longer held.) Sometimes, however, a sport's inclusion as a demonstration event led to medal status in later Olympic Games. So it was with freestyle skiing.

All three forms of freestyle skiing—moguls, aerials, and ballet—were demonstrated at the 1988 Calgary Olympics. In 1992, moguls became a medal event. In this event, skiers race over a course of moguls, or snow bumps. They must complete high-speed turns and perform two stunts in the air during their downhill run.

In 1994, freestyle aerial skiing was added as a medal event. Aerial skiing is similar to the ski jump, except that competitors perform stunts while in the air.

New to the medal events at the 1998 Nagano Olympics will be snowboarding. A snowboard is a wide, single ski to

which both feet are attached. Men and women will compete in separate giant slalom and half-pipe events. A half-pipe is a U-shaped trough dug in the snow. Snowboarders use a half-pipe to perform aerial stunts and acrobatic maneuvers.

Skating and Ice Hockey

Skating is one of the most popular events at the Olympics. Dressed in beautiful costumes, skaters perform complicated and demanding routines. They are judged by their grace and their ability to jump and spin. People enjoy the artistry and style of the dancers.

Both singles (top) and pairs (bottom) figure skating are beautiful examples of grace and athleticism.

Speed skating demands enormous energy and skill.

There is another skating event, however, that hasn't received much attention: speed skating. It's not a flashy, artistic sport like figure skating. Speed skaters race around an oval track. The skater with the best time wins.

Ice hockey is a fast-moving and exciting sport. Teams put five players and a goalie on the ice at one time. Coaches keep their players fresh by

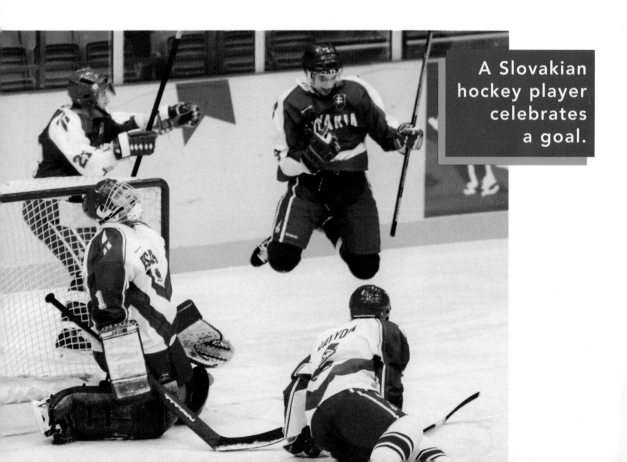

A Slovakian hockey player celebrates a goal.

substituting them every few minutes. Canada and Russia (formerly the Soviet Union) have captured most of the gold medals since ice hockey's first Olympic appearance in 1920.

Curling is a sport that resembles shuffleboard on ice. Taking turns, team members use sticks to push large stones across the ice to a circular goal, called the "house." First seen as a demonstration event

A curling area resembles a giant shuffleboard made of ice (left). Curling players try to control the speed and direction of the "stone" (above).

in 1924, it will be a medal event at the 1998 Nagano Olympics.

Ice Dancing

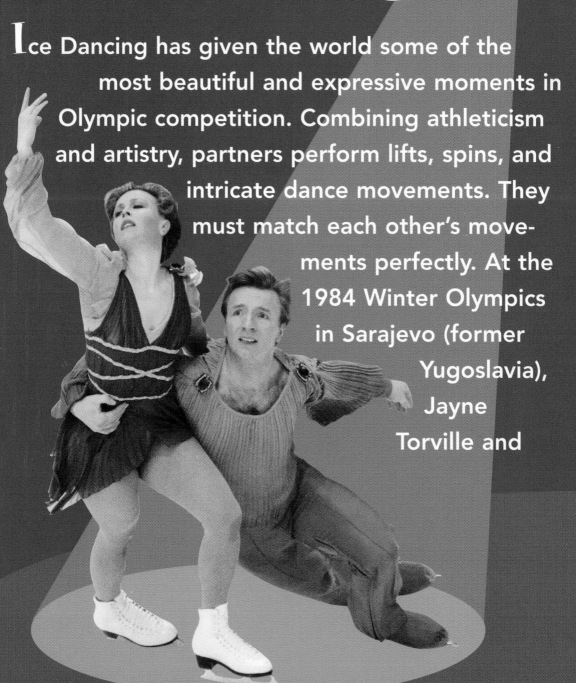

Ice Dancing has given the world some of the most beautiful and expressive moments in Olympic competition. Combining athleticism and artistry, partners perform lifts, spins, and intricate dance movements. They must match each other's movements perfectly. At the 1984 Winter Olympics in Sarajevo (former Yugoslavia), Jayne Torville and

Christopher Dean of Great Britain gave an unforgettable performance. They are one of the few pairs in history to receive a perfect score. Recent performances by exciting new couples insure that ice dancing will remain one of the most popular events at the Winter Olympics.

These two couples demonstrate the wide range in styles of ice dance. Torville and Dean (left) are slow and passionate, Gritchtuck and Platov (right) are fast and exciting.

Bobsledding and the Luge

Riding a bobsled down an icy chute, or bob-run, is like riding a speeding rocket. Invented in the 1880s, the first sleds were wooden. To gain speed, the two- and four-man teams leaned back and jerked forward. This motion is called "bobbing,"

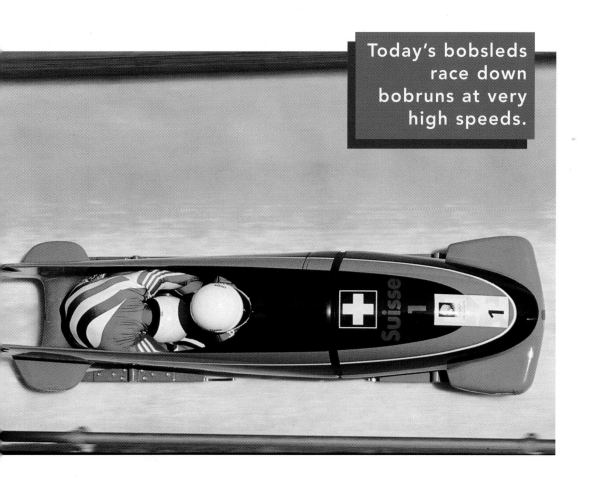

Today's bobsleds race down bobruns at very high speeds.

and it gives the sport its name.

Today, bobsledders no longer "bob." They ride in fiberglass and steel sleds that hurtle along at blinding speeds. They can reach 100 miles per hour (160 kilometers per hour) and more on a straightaway. From start to finish, the ride may take less than a minute.

Lugeing, or tobogganing, is one of the most dangerous sports in the Olympics. Contestants, known as "sliders," lie on their backs. They zoom feet-first down a steep, ice-covered track. Like bob-

The luge is one of the fastest events in the Olympics.

sledding, it may take a minute or less to go from the starting gate to the finish line.

Men compete either as singles or, on a two-seater luge sled, as doubles. Women compete only in a singles event.

The Spirit of the Winter Olympics

Although set in frozen ice and snow, the atmosphere at the Winter Olympics is one of festive enjoyment. Visitors and fans brave the cold to cheer on their favorite athletes. Athletes gather in the Olympic village to swap stories and make new friends.

Left: Nancy Kerrigan, Oksana Baiul, and Lu Chin (left-to-right), stand arm in arm after winning the silver, gold, and bronze medals in the figure skating competition. Right: A cheerful Norwegian spectator.

They understand that the Olympic spirit does not exist only in competition and winning. It exists as an idea that people and nations can unite to compete in friendship and harmony.

To Find Out More

Here are some additional resources to help you learn more about the Winter Olympics:

 **Books**

 **Organizations**

Duden, Jane. **The Olympics.** Macmillan Child Group, 1991.

Greenspan, Bud. **100 Greatest Moments in Olympic History.** General Publishing Group, 1995.

Harris, Jack C. **The Winter Olympics.** Creative Education, Inc., 1990.

Haycock, Kate. **Skiing.** Crestwood House, 1991.

Malley, Stephen. **A Kid's Guide to the Nineteen Ninety-Four Winter Olympics.** Bantam Press, 1994.

Wallechinsky, David. **The Complete Book of the Winter Olympics.** Little, Brown & Co., 1993.

U.S. Biathlon Association (USBA)
421 Old Military Road
Lake Placid, NY 12946

U.S. Bobsled and Skeleton Federation (UBSF)
P.O. Box 828
Lake Placid, NY 12946

United States Figure Skating Association
20 First Street
Colorado Springs, CO 80906

United States International Speedskating Association
P.O. Box 16157
Rocky River, OH 44116

U.S. Skiing (USSA)
P.O. Box 100
Park City, UT 84060

Online Sites

2002 Winter Olympic Games Home Page
www.SLC2002.org

A growing web page that provides information on the 2002 Winter Olympics in Salt Lake City.

Official 1998 Olympic Web Site
www.nagano.olympic.org

A great source of information on the events of the 1998 Winter Olympics.

An Olympic Games Primer
www.aafla.com/pubs/ olyprim.htm

An exciting site that introduces the Olympic games.

Original Luge Home Page
www.luge.com

Learn about the different equipment and techniques necessary to ride the luge.

Winter Sports Page
www.wintersports.org

A central site to explore winter sports and links to other sites.

Important Words

aerial stunts performed in the air

Alpine skiing downhill skiing

emblem a design that represents something else

gates flags that indicate turns to slalom skiers

half-pipe a U-shaped trench that snowboarders use for performing stunts and acrobatics

moguls bumps made of snow

Nordic skiing cross-country skiing that includes courses that run downhill, as well as through meadows and woods

symbol an object that represents another thing or idea

Index

Meet the Author

Larry Dane Brimner is the author of several books for Children's Press, including five True Books on the Winter Olympics. He is a member of the Authors Guild and the Society of Children's Book Writers and Illustrators. Mr. Brimner makes his home in Southern California and the Rocky Mountains.